What Educators are Saying about The EQed Classroom

"I loved everything about this book! Every educator needs The EQed Classroom. This book addresses the real challenges we face in schools today and offers actionable strategies. The "See Me Framework" is a game-changer—that should be posted in every classroom to remind us of the importance of truly seeing and valuing our students.

It's perfect for campus or district-wide book studies. The EQed Classroom is the guide we've been waiting for to create classrooms where social and emotional learning skills are developed and where emotional intelligence drives connection, equity, and success."

Dr. Diane Newton
RRS Federal Programs Director
3rd-12th Principal

"The strategies in this book are simple but powerful and all too often easily forgotten. I believe this book applies to all levels of the teaching experience and provides a solid framework for building relationships and classroom culture. This book is needed in every classroom."

Zahkeya Dixon
2024 LPSS Middle School Teacher of the Year

"Comprehension is significantly influenced by individual experiences. As a former classroom teacher, curriculum specialist, and currently an assistant principal, I have witnessed the effectiveness of Emotional Intelligence (EQ) in various educational roles. The ability to connect, communicate, and collaborate is essential for success in education.

The framework provided in The EQed Classroom: Leveraging Self-Awareness to Create Engaging Environments aligns with Louisiana's recently adopted National Institute for Excellence in Teaching (NIET) evaluation system. The framework can serve as a valuable tool for enhancing and supporting aspects of the domains of "instruction," "planning," "environment," and "professionalism." This includes, but is not limited to, *strategies for student grouping, motivating students, understanding students' needs, developing instructional plans, engaging students, managing behavior, fostering respectful conditions, setting expectations, growing and developing professionally, and reflecting on teaching practices."*

Kayla Joseph Jones
SLPSB Assistant Principal
2022 Louisiana Teacher of the Year Semi-finalist

"Being self-aware and having emotional intelligence is a key factor to being a successful educator. The author gave an exceptional depiction of emotional intelligence with key examples that made me reflect on ways to improve my EQ."

Tommy Jones
Assistant Principal
Former EPSB District SEL Coordinator

"Educators expect student outcomes. We want students to produce, but how we show up influences those outcomes. The EQed Classroom: Leveraging Self-Awareness….addresses the need for EQ in the classroom. By focusing on educating the whole child—academically, socially, and emotionally—we can directly impact student achievement in meaningful ways. Frederick Douglass said, "It's easier to build strong children than to repair broken men.""

Octavia Warren
Central Middle School Principal
2024 SLPSB Middle School Principal of the Year

"This book should be in the hands of and available to every novice educator. It should be used as a basis for in-service at the beginning of each school year. Everything else can take a backseat the first week of school."

Gwen Lewis
Retired Principal

THE EQED CLASSROOM

Leveraging Self-Awareness to Create Engaging Environments

Dr. Phyllis Donatto

Copyright © 2024 Dr. Phyllis Donatto
All rights reserved.

No part of this book may be reproduced, stored in a retrieval system, or transmitted in any form or by any means—electronic, mechanical, photocopying, recording, or otherwise—without prior written permission from the author, except for brief quotations in reviews or critical articles.

Paperback ISBN 979-8-9892137-8-8
eBook ISBN 979-8-9892137-9-5

Published by FTH Dimension Solutions

First Edition: 2024

Cover Design: Ese Osakwe

For permissions, inquiries, or bulk orders, contact info@fthdimensions.com.

TABLE OF CONTENTS

Foreword 11

Dedication 15

Introduction 17

Chapter 1: The Need for EQ in the Classroom 19

Chapter 2: The Role of Self-Awareness in EQ 31

Chapter 3: C³ Key Principles™ 41

Chapter 4: Using the C³ Key Principles™ for Disruptive Behavior ... 53

Chapter 5: C³ EQed Classroom Resources 67

Chapter 6: SEL and Equity 79

Conclusion 83

About the Author 87

Appendix 91

    The Power C Chart™ 92

    Benefits of CASEL Competencies 93

        Self-Awareness 93

        Self-Management 94

        Social Awareness 95

        Responsible Decision-Making 96

        Relationship Skills 97

C³ Key Principles™ EQed Implementation Management Plan 99

Sources 101

FOREWORD

Having known Dr. Phyllis Donatto for nearly three decades, I often find myself reflecting on the moment we first met—it feels like it was just yesterday. Back then, she was an ambitious undergraduate conducting a qualitative research project, and I was the Director of Student Development. We had just wrapped up a lengthy conversation about whether she should join *our* sorority—yes, *our sorority*. That conversation marked the start of a lifelong bond, one that has only deepened and grown stronger with each passing year. Not long after, I transitioned from the university back to the local school district as the Personnel Director, and wouldn't you know it, Dr. Donatto began her teaching career at the very same school where I had started mine. Watching her journey from that first-year teacher to where she is today has been truly inspiring. Over the years, her career has flourished—from teacher to school administrator, to university professor, and beyond. She's served on state appointed committees, including one appointed by the governor, contributed as a coauthor of a statewide adopted alternative teacher certification curriculum, written her own leadership curriculum for teens, and developed online courses to take teachers and students on a journey of self-discovery and empowerment to increase their self-awareness, manage their emotions, and build strong relationships.

Prior to launching out on her own, Dr. Donatto worked as a leadership development strategist for a national education training company, where she coached and trained district and campus administrators, teachers, and staff. Driven by a desire to chart her own path and make an even greater impact during COVID, Dr. Donatto started FTH Dimension Solutions. In writing this book, Dr. Donatto entices us with the title alone: Using self-awareness (that is, the realization or understanding of oneself) to create environments that are engaging (i.e., environments that are connected, collaborative, and safe). Dr. Donatto approaches one of the five core competencies of Social and Emotional Learning (SEL), self-awareness, as described by CASEL (Collaborative for Academic, Social, and Emotional Learning), who says that "these competencies can be taught and applied… across diverse cultural contexts, to articulate what is helpful to know and be able to do for academic success, school and civic engagement, health and wellness, and fulfilling careers." Dr. Donatto's approach offers a practical and transformative perspective on fostering these essential skills.

Dr. Donatto brings to the forefront how emotional intelligence and social and emotional learning relate to workplace relationships, teamwork, and school climate and culture, emphasizing that while emotional intelligence (EQ) and SEL are similar, they are different. Dr. Donatto challenges educators to reflect upon their own emotional intelligence to see how it affects their ability to build trust, show empathy, address conflict, and model self-control, as each of these impacts students' engagement, motivation, and willingness to learn. This is a MUST read, particularly for those who are looking for something different, something to change the trajectory of their educational prowess.

Daphene O. Singleton, Ph.D.

Educational Consultant | HR Professional

DEDICATION

This book is dedicated to the most impactful group of individuals I know, Teachers.

"I have come to the frightening conclusion that I am the decisive element. It is my personal approach that creates the climate. It is my daily mood that makes the weather. I possess tremendous power to make life miserable or joyous. I can be a tool of torture or an instrument of inspiration, I can humiliate or humor, hurt or heal. In all situations, it is my response that decides whether a crisis is escalated or de-escalated, and a person is humanized or de-humanized. If we treat people as they are, we make them worse. If we treat people as they ought to be, we help them become what they are capable of becoming." **Haim G. Ginott**

Thank you for showing up each and every day and making a difference in the lives of our students.

With heartfelt gratitude,

Dr. Phyllis Donatto

Introduction

Teaching is more than a profession—it's a charge to make a positive impact by influencing, inspiring lives, and leading others in ways that position them for success in school and beyond.

This book is a guide for educators who are not only committed to teaching academic content but also to shaping the emotional and social lives of their students. In today's classrooms, the role of a teacher extends far beyond delivering lessons—it involves fostering connections, building trust, and creating a safe and supportive environment where students can thrive academically, emotionally, and socially.

In this book, you'll explore the critical role EQ plays in creating engaging environments. Through practical strategies, reflective exercises, and relatable examples, you'll learn how to integrate the principles of emotional intelligence into your teaching. You'll discover how to build trust through connection, foster clarity through communication, and empower students through collaboration—the three pillars of what I call the C³ Key Principles™.

Each chapter delves deeper into these principles, offering tools and insights to help you create positive, welcoming environments. Whether you're a new teacher looking to establish strong foundations or a seasoned educator seeking fresh approaches, *The EQed Classroom: Leveraging Self-Awareness to Create Engaging Environments* can help you create classrooms where connection, communication, and collaboration thrive.

CHAPTER ONE

THE NEED FOR EQ IN THE CLASSROOM

> *"Your emotions influence your thoughts. Your thoughts influence your behavior, and your behavior influences the outcome of your interactions."*
> **- Dr. Phyllis Donatto**

"You catch more flies with honey than with vinegar." This was just one of the many wise sayings my parents would say as I was growing up. I'm sure you've heard the same thing or something similar. I was also taught to smile—a universal language of kindness—say thank you, make eye contact, and always respond when someone speaks to me. Respect was a non-negotiable: "Yes, Ma'am," and "No, Sir," were the first part of any response when answering a question, if not the complete sentence.

These lessons were so engrained in me that when I stepped into the classroom as a first-year teacher in 1996, they were a natural part of my interaction with my students. At the time, I didn't fully realize that these habits were more than good manners—they were foundational elements of emotional intelligence. Without even knowing the term, I was leveraging skills like empathy, self-regulation, and social awareness to create a positive classroom environment. While there were occasional disruptions, as there are in any classroom, I found that redirecting inappropriate behavior was not as challenging.

In recent years, emotional intelligence and social and emotional learning have been at the forefront of many conversations about workplace relationships, high-performing teams, and climate and culture, and rightfully so. Emotional and social competence are essential skills for building community and creating engaging environments. These critical life skills have profound implications in the classroom and beyond, and while research has always supported this fact, more and more of society is starting to realize the importance of emotional intelligence, especially after "the great interruption" (at least, that's what I called it) of COVID-19 in 2020. The crisis interrupted our total way of existing.

The after-effects of COVID-19 brought the conversation about emotional intelligence back to the forefront. Not only did the disease attack our physical bodies, but it also attacked our ability to form connections, communicate effectively, and show empathy. Many are still struggling in these areas as these challenges have increased anxiety, eroded trust, and revealed the inability of some to self-manage — effects that are now clearly visible in classrooms nationwide.

Success in any area of life requires more than book smarts. It requires what some call self-smart and others call emotion-smart. Both imply the need for something more than intelligence (IQ) to experience success in our personal and professional lives.

Daniel Goleman, the author of the 1995 classic <u>Emotional Intelligence</u>, wrote, *"Emotional intelligence is the key to both personal and professional success. It is not the smartest who achieve the most, but those who can manage their emotions and the emotions of others with grace, empathy, and wisdom."*

Emotional Intelligence

What is emotional intelligence? There are several definitions, including this one.

> Emotional Intelligence, EQ, is the ability to recognize, understand, and manage our own emotions and recognize, understand, and influence the emotions of others. In short, emotional intelligence (EQ) is understanding and managing emotions—yours and others.

For educators, possessing emotional intelligence is vital to creating engaging environments where students can thrive academically, socially, and emotionally. It is the cornerstone for personal growth that extends well beyond the classroom, influencing and impacting students' success for years to come.

This is why a teacher's ability to build connections with students, engage in clear empathetic communication, and foster collaboration among students is vital to the learning process. Generally speaking, the higher the level of emotional intelligence, the better the chances that the teacher will possess stronger classroom management skills.

Classroom management can be challenging, and it is also the area where EQ can have the most significant impact. A teacher with emotional intelligence is more likely to be able to redirect misbehavior in a non-threatening way by addressing the issue without unintentionally devaluing the student, thus creating engaging, safe, supportive environments where students feel valued, understood, engaged, and motivated to learn.

Social and Emotional Learning (SEL) Competencies

While emotional intelligence and SEL are similar, they are different. SEL focuses on skill development, while EQ is about understanding and managing emotions.

Think of it this way: EQ allows you to apply the SEL skills you have learned.

CASEL, the Collaborative for Academic, Social, and Emotional Learning, a leading organization dedicated to advancing social and emotional learning in schools, purports that integrating SEL practices into education supports students' development in self-awareness, self-management, social awareness, relationship skills, and responsible decision-making all of which align with what I have coined as the *C³ Key Principles™: Connection, Communication, and Collaboration.*

CASEL's Core Competencies of Social and Emotional Learning (SEL) are essential life skills that promote positive behavior and mental well-being and help students succeed in school and beyond. These competencies are as follows:

1. **Self-Awareness:** Understanding one's emotions, thoughts, and values and how they influence behavior. This includes accurately assessing one's strengths and limitations. It is crucial because it

helps individuals build confidence and a realistic sense of self.

2. **Self-Management:** The ability to regulate emotions, thoughts, and behaviors in different situations. It includes managing stress, controlling impulses, and setting and working toward personal goals. Effective self-management is vital for resilience and achieving personal and academic success.

3. **Social Awareness:** Understanding and empathizing with others, including those from diverse backgrounds and cultures. It also involves recognizing social norms and understanding ethical behaviors. Social awareness fosters inclusivity and respect for others.

4. **Relationship Skills:** The ability to establish and maintain healthy and rewarding relationships, which involves clear communication, active listening, cooperation, and conflict resolution. Strong relationship skills are essential for teamwork and building supportive networks.

5. **Responsible Decision-Making:** The ability to make caring and constructive choices about personal behavior and social interactions. It requires consideration of ethical standards, safety, and the well-being of others. Good decision-making promotes accountability and helps individuals navigate challenges responsibly.

Collaborative for Academic, Social, and Emotional Learning (CASEL). (2023). *Core SEL Competencies.* Retrieved from https://casel.org/sel-framework/

The benefits of building strong connections in the classroom include both social and academic benefits. A research study by Durlak and others revealed that students who participated in social and emotional learning programs showed significant academic improvement. One could also make the case that students exposed to teachers with higher levels of emotional intelligence who consistently model SEL skills, are likely to repeat the behavior patterns, actions, and interactions they experience. If this is the case—and I believe it is—then a teacher's behavior can speak and teach much more than words alone.

A teacher's emotional intelligence affects their ability to build trust, show empathy, address conflict, and model self-control. Each of these impacts students' engagement, motivation, and willingness to participate in learning activities. When students feel connected to their teacher, they are more likely to take risks, ask questions, and push through challenges (i.e., hard things). I strongly advocate for educators to continually grow and develop their personal and social competencies. Not only can it help with classroom management, but the added benefit is that it models appropriate EQ for students as they learn and develop social and emotional learning skills.

Benefits of Social and Emotional Learning

As you can see there are several benefits of your students possessing these SEL Skills. Not only do they help with classroom management, but they position students for success by learning fundamental leadership skills that will serve them well in their future careers and relationships. Fill in the chart on the next page with the benefits of your students possessing SEL Skills and their impact on the teaching and learning experience in your classroom. An example has been provided in each area to help you get started.

Benefits of SEL Chart

SEL SKILL	*If my students possessed this skill, what behaviors might occur more often?*	*If my students possessed this skill, what behaviors might occur less often?*
Self-Awareness	• Showing confidence • •	• Being defensive when being redirected • •
Self-Management	• Listening • •	• Less blurting out • •
Social Awareness	• Being kind • •	• Making fun of others • •
Relationship Skills	• Helping classmates • •	• Arguing • •
Responsible Decision-Making	• Completing assignments • •	• Blaming others • •

SEL skills not only help to improve classroom management by creating engaging learning environments, but they also empower students with tools for success beyond academics.

These benefits are not exclusive to students; they apply to adults, as well. SEL skills are essential in personal and professional success at any stage of life. A one-page summary of the benefits of possessing each of these skills and ways to grow them is located in the Appendix.

Chapter One Key Takeaways

1. Emotional Intelligence (EQ) plays a vital role in creating engaging environments.

2. Emotional Intelligence and Social and Emotional Learning (SEL) are similar but not the same. EQ focuses on managing emotions, and SEL emphasizes skill development.

3. Growing your EQ can help improve your relationships with students and model appropriate SEL skills.

Reflection Exercise

Ask Yourself:

- How self-aware am I of my behaviors, actions, and interactions with my students?

- In challenging moments with my students, how do I typically respond?

- Do my students see me as approachable, or do I unintentionally engage in behaviors, actions, and interactions that send signals that suggest that I am unapproachable?

CHAPTER TWO

THE ROLE OF SELF-AWARENESS IN EQ

> *"To Thine Ownself be True."*
> **- Hamlet**

When seeking strategies to improve classroom management, ways to deal with distributive behaviors or dealing with difficult students, the last place most educators tend to look is at themselves. In reality, it should be one of the first. This is because the success of any program depends on the individual's ability to deliver it effectively, and a person's level of self-awareness will serve as an influential factor.

Self-awareness is the bedrock of emotional intelligence (EQ) and involves understanding your emotions, behaviors, and their impact on others. For teachers, self-awareness means recognizing how your emotional state impacts the classroom environment. It's about knowing your strengths and constraints, understanding what pushes your buttons, and reflecting on appropriate responses that demonstrate value while communicating the desired expectation or outcome in the classroom setting.

When teachers can regulate their own emotions and respond to students with empathy and clarity, they foster a sense of belonging in the classroom and create a safe space for respect, kindness, and mutual understanding to become the norm and not the exception. They create spaces and places where students want to be. Furthermore, research suggests that psychologically safe classrooms often experience fewer problems, which helps to reduce behavioral issues and improves the overall teaching and learning experience.

Being self-aware means having a clear understanding of your thoughts and emotions in the present moment. This is important for teachers because your emotions influence how you behave in your interactions with your students. This can make all the difference in getting a student to comply. It can also provoke semi-defiant and/or defiant behavior, especially if a student is dealing with trauma. Generally speaking, teachers who may want to consider the need for growth in this area often find themselves yelling unnecessarily or overreacting when addressing inappropriate behavior.

An example of overreacting may be sending a student out of the classroom for talking when they should be working or raising your voice without cause (i.e., threat of danger) when redirecting inappropriate behavior. This example is not intended to minimize a teacher's legitimate frustration when addressing off-task behavior, especially when they, too, may be experiencing trauma. Instead, it suggests that their rising frustration may add to the problem.

Self-awareness is a powerful tool because the ability to engage in meaningful connection starts here. The teacher's self-awareness, or lack thereof, shapes the classroom dynamics and influences students' learning experiences.

There are several ways to assess your level of self-awareness. This includes reflecting on interactions, asking for feedback, and paying attention to your responses and interactions with others. Another more in-depth way is to complete an emotional intelligence assessment.

An EQ assessment can reveal your personal and social competencies. It can highlight areas of strength while identifying potential areas for growth. Not only can increasing your self-awareness help create a more engaging classroom environment for you and your students, but it can also help improve your personal relationships and professional effectiveness.

The emotional awareness questions on the next page are not intended to provide any type of diagnosis, medical or otherwise, and should not be used to draw conclusions about a person's level of emotional awareness. Rather, they serve as a self-reflection tool ONLY, to initiate self-exploration about emotional intelligence.

For each statement about emotions, reflect on your awareness and respond with "Yes," "No," or "Sometimes."

	I am aware of how I am feeling at any given moment.
	I can recognize subtle shifts in my mood during the day.
	Emotions play an important part in my life.
	I am aware of how my mood impacts the people around me.
	I am aware of when others' moods are impacting me.
	I take intentional mood checks throughout the day.
	It is easy for me to describe my feelings.
	I tell others my true feelings.
	I think before acting or responding, especially when I am upset.
	I notice how my body responds to certain emotions (e.g., tension).
	____Total # of **Yes** ____Total # of **Sometimes** ____Total # of **No**

Reflection Exercise

Celebrate the area(s) where you answered "Yes."

Ask Yourself:

- What experiences have helped me reach this stage?

- How often am I sharing or modeling those experiences with my students?

- What is one thing I can do to help my students grow in this area?

- What resources are currently available, and what other resources do I need to help my students grow in this area?

For the area(s) where you answered "Sometimes," reflect on what causes the inconsistency.

Ask Yourself:

- What conditions make it challenging for me to be consistent?

- What time of day is it more challenging?

For the area(s) where you answered "No," choose one area of growth.

Ask Yourself:

- Which area do I want to focus on first?
- What might make it hard for me to do this?
- What can I do to overcome this obstacle?

It is important to note that, as with anything, growing your EQ is a process. Change takes time and a commitment to the process.

Developing and growing in self-awareness is a continuous process that requires intentional reflection. Setting aside time to reflect on your emotions, behaviors, and teaching practices allows you to gain deeper insights into how you "show up" in the classroom and how your presence affects your students.

Chapter Two Key Takeaways

1. Your emotions play a huge role in shaping your classroom environment.

2. Engaging in intentional reflective practices helps grow self-awareness.

3. Self-awareness enhances personal relationships and professional effectiveness.

Reflection Exercise

Ask Yourself:

- How do my behaviors, actions, and interactions influence my students' behaviors?

- Who can I ask for honest feedback about my behaviors and interactions with my students?

- What time during the instructional day do I most need to pause and do a mental check-in?

CHAPTER THREE

C³ Key Principles™

Connection, Communication, and Collaboration

> *"Connect, communicate, and collaborate with others in ways that positively impact your life and the lives of others."*
> **- Dr. Phyllis Donatto**

The ability to connect, communicate, and collaborate influences a person's personal and professional success. In the classroom, the ability to connect, communicate, and collaborate is what stands between a teacher experiencing more calm or chaotic moments. It is my personal belief that these three areas bear witness to a person's personal and social competency.

Emotionally intelligent individuals engage more effectively in each of these three areas in ways that yield positive outcomes and influence others. Because of the interconnectedness of the terms, I refer to them as the C³ Key Principles™. Taken together, these terms create a synergistic process where connection helps to build trust. Trust resulting from connection makes it easier to communicate, and clear communication provides clarity, resulting in the likelihood of shared goals, which strengthens collaboration. This simple but powerful approach displays EQ in full effect and creates meaningful interactions in the classroom and beyond.

Let's take a closer look at each of these principles.

The Connection Key ⚬━

Let's start with the first C in the C³ Key Principles™, connection. Connection is the cornerstone of any productive and supportive classroom environment. Connection refers to the emotional bond between the teacher and students, and it's built through trust, understanding, and positive interactions.

In classrooms where teachers prioritize connection, students feel valued and recognized, which enhances their engagement and willingness to participate in learning. Research shows that students who have strong, positive connections with their teachers are more likely to feel emotionally safe, take risks (i.e., try or make an effort), and develop appropriate social and emotional learning skills.

For teachers, building relational capacity—the ability to form meaningful connections with students, shapes the overall climate of the classroom. Strong connections create an atmosphere where students feel comfortable, and when students are comfortable, they can thrive emotionally, academically, and personally.

The SEE ME Framework™ is a simple yet powerful tool for building strong, lasting connections with students, and it all starts with engagement.

The SEE ME Framework™

- **Smile:** A smile is a quick, easy way to connect, and it makes you seem approachable.

- **Eye Contact:** Making eye contact is often thought of as conveying respect and attention and a way of expressing interest. *Note, that this is not universal. In some cultures, making eye contact is a sign of disrespect. Make sure you know your students.* The intent is to notice your students.

- **Engaged Body Language:** An open, relaxed posture conveys openness. Be mindful of multi-tasking when engaging with students. This might unintentionally communicate disinterest.

- **Mindful Tone:** You have heard it before, "It's not what you say, but how you say it." Your tone speaks volumes. Even in conflict, maintaining a calm, caring tone helps keep the environment safe.

- **Empathy:** Be willing to listen and validate your students' feelings and concerns, even if you don't share that same experience. Their experiences are real for them.

Reflection Exercise

Rate yourself on the SEE ME Framework™ on a scale of one to three, with three (3) being *often*, two (2) being *sometimes*, and one (1) being *I need to do this more*.

- How often do I smile at my students?

- How often do I really notice (i.e., truly see) my students?

- How open and engaging is my body language?

- How mindful am I of my tone when interacting with my students, especially in challenging situations?

- How often do I actively practice empathy with my students?

The Communication Key ⚬—┯

The second principle in the C³ Key Principles™ is communication. Communication is the heart of every classroom interaction. It is the cornerstone of a teacher's ability to inspire, educate, and guide their students. Communication is more than just sharing information, giving directions, and stating expectations; it includes listening and showing empathy. It serves as the foundation for building relationships.

Students want to feel heard, and when teachers actively listen to their students' thoughts, ideas, and concerns, it builds trust and strengthens relationships. Active listening demonstrates respect and shows students that their concerns, opinions, and experiences matter, too.

In classrooms where communication is clear and open, students are more engaged and feel more comfortable participating. They understand the expectations placed on them, and they are more likely to ask questions, seek help when needed, and collaborate with their peers. Effective communication is essential in creating engaging environments that support academic achievement and emotional safety. Here are some strategies you can use to help ensure your students feel heard and understood:

- Listen without interrupting them when they are speaking, and acknowledge their perspectives.

- It seems simple enough, but really hone in on what they are saying when talking to them and resist the urge to finish their sentences. If you ask them a question, allow them to answer. 😊

- Be fully present.
  - Give your students your full attention, and be mindful of your body language, facial expressions, and tone. Your non-verbal cues matter. Sometimes, they can speak louder than your words.

- Check for understanding with intentional responses.
  - Say back what you think you heard. For example, "So, what I hear you saying is…. Is that right?"

- Communicate with clarity.
  - Be clear about what's expected. Write it down if you must. Remember, "What's in your head has to be said." 😊

Reflection Exercise

Ask Yourself:

- How often do I truly listen to my students without interrupting?

- Do students feel comfortable approaching me with questions or concerns?

- How mindful am I of my tone when speaking with students?

The Collaboration Key

The third principle in the C³ Key Principles™ is collaboration. It teaches students how to work with others, resolve conflict, and communicate effectively, all of which are essential life skills.

Creating a collaborative classroom is more than having students work together on projects. It's about fostering a culture where students feel empowered to contribute, their voices are heard, and they share in the learning experience. Collaboration allows students to share their ideas and perspectives when working together. This interaction can spark creativity and encourage critical thinking.

One of the most effective ways to foster collaboration is by providing opportunities for students to lead. Giving students opportunities to lead and offering them choices is how they learn essential collaboration skills. When students are given a voice and have a choice in their learning experience, they take ownership of their learning. When students feel ownership of their learning and work together to achieve shared goals, it not only deepens their understanding of the material but also helps them develop social and emotional skills that will serve them throughout their lives.

Collaboration fosters a learning community where everyone's voice matters. This is an important social awareness attribute. Collaboration activities provide leadership opportunities for students. Participating in these experiences helps strengthen their communication skills, helps them build confidence, and prepares them for the real world. These experiences also contribute to their social and emotional development.

When planning for students to work together in groups, there are some key elements to consider. Here is a list of best practices when planning for group collaboration:

- Set Clear Expectations
    - Before starting a collaborative project, set clear expectations for behavior, participation, and outcomes. Establish guidelines for respectful communication, active listening, and equal contribution from all members.

- Teach Collaboration Skills
    - Show students how to work together. Role-play listening, giving feedback, and conflict resolution. Students don't automatically know how to collaborate effectively.

- Assign Group Roles
    - Assigning roles provides structure by ensuring everyone knows their role and job. Roles can include scribe, reporter, timekeeper, and facilitator, to name a few.

- Actively Monitor

    o As students work in groups, walk around the room to monitor their progress and provide support, as needed.

Chapter Three Key Takeaways

1. The C³ Key Principles™ create a synergy where connection builds trust, communication helps with understanding, and collaboration strengthens bonds that shape the overall climate of the classroom.

2. The SEE ME Framework™ provides a practical framework for teachers to build relationships and develop trust.

3. Effective collaboration in the classroom not only deepens students' understanding of academic material but also develops their social skills, empathy, and respect for diverse perspectives.

Reflection Exercise

Ask Yourself:

- How well do I currently incorporate the SEE ME Framework™ in my daily interactions with students, and in what areas can I improve?

- How can I adjust my communication to ensure I am actively listening and providing clarity to support my students?

- What steps can I take to create a more collaborative environment that empowers students to take ownership of their learning?

CHAPTER FOUR

USING THE C³ KEY PRINCIPLES™ FOR DISRUPTIVE BEHAVIOR

> *"Kind words are like honey, sweet to the body and healthy for the soul."*
> *- African Proverb*

Most educators would agree that addressing disciplinary issues and classroom management are two of the most challenging aspects of teaching. Disruptive behavior not only hinders the teacher's right to teach, but it also hinders students' right to learn. Excessive disruptive behavior can also lead to anxiety and frustration for teachers and students, leading to poor student performance, teacher stress, and burnout. Here lies the case for emotional intelligence for teachers.

Emotional intelligence can help teachers create classroom environments where meaningful learning takes place and everyone thrives, making the teaching experience a rewarding career that impacts and influences the lives of children, which is what most teachers signed up for when they first entered the profession.

The C³ Key Principles™—Connection, Communication, and Collaboration— discussed in the previous chapter provide an effective strategy for dealing with off-task and inappropriate behavior. The tool can help create classroom environments where redirecting disruptive behavior is an opportunity for personal growth for everyone involved and can transform how teachers and students experience disciplinary moments. For the teacher, it provides a respectful approach to redirecting inappropriate behavior, reducing stress and frustration. For the students, it models emotional intelligence and demonstrates a positive way to address conflict resolution while reinforcing a culture of respect. The C³ Key Principles™ also help students understand the impact of their actions and interactions and encourages them to take part in positive behavior change with their dignity intact.

The primary goal in using the C³ Key Principles™ when addressing off-task and inappropriate behavior is to create a dialogue for shared problem-solving between the teacher and the student where emotions are managed and relationships remain intact. The following scenarios offer examples of how to apply the C³ Key Principles™ as a classroom management strategy to create positive outcomes for you and your students.

Scenario 1: A Student Disrupts the Class

1. Connection:

Pause and take a deep breath. Resist the urge to show your frustration, make eye contact with the student, calmly address them by name to acknowledge their presence, and bring attention to the disruption.

2. Communicate:

Address the behavior in a clear, non-confrontational way. You might say, "I noticed you're talking while I'm teaching. Is there something you need or that I can help you with? We want everyone to benefit from the lesson, so let's stay focused." This calm interaction reminds the student of expectations in a non-threatening or shaming manner.

3. Collaboration:

Later during class or after class, check in with the student individually. Let them know you want the best for them in and outside the classroom and that you are there to help.

Scenario 2: A Student Becomes Frustrated with Their Work

1. Connection:

Being mindful of your body language and tone, approach the student and say, "It looks as if you are frustrated or having a hard time with this assignment. Where is it confusing for you, or where are you getting stuck?" This approach shows care and concern while acknowledging their struggle.

2. Communication:

Tell the student that you are there to help. Say, "Let's look at it together." Ask, "What do we need to do first?" This communicates that you want to help, which can help lower the student's anxiety.

3. Collaboration:

Explain to the student that you know how frustrating it is when you don't understand something. Share a time when you did not understand something and became frustrated. Explain how you handled the situation. Ask the student what they can do the next time they feel frustrated. This approach models emotional management and gives the student an idea of how to handle a similar situation in the future.

Scenario 3: A Student Engages in Name Calling

1. Connection:

Approach the student calmly and ask them to step near the door or away from the other students. Ask, "What happened to you?" "I overheard what you just said. Let's talk about what's going on." This non-judgmental approach creates an opportunity for the student to open up.

2. Communicate:

Be mindful of your tone. Say, "I want all of us in this class to feel respected. Calling someone out of their name hurts that person, and it can affect those who overheard it, which makes our class not feel like a safe space. Our classroom is a safe space."

3. Collaboration:

Ask, "What do you need to do moving forward when tempted to call someone else out of their name? How can you make this right and ensure it doesn't happen again?" Thank the student for listening. Then, explain that everyone makes mistakes and that what's important is to learn from them and not repeat them. This approach helps to build trust, communicates care and concern for the student, allows the student to own their behavior, and equips them with responsible decision-making skills.

Scenario 4: Addressing Tardiness

1. **Connection:**

    Greet the student by name at the door or allow them to be seated. Tell them you are glad they made it to class and ask if everything is okay. This lets the student know you see them first rather than communicating the issue first.

2. **Communication:**

    Be mindful of your tone and body language; remind the student when the class starts. Say, "Remember, the class starts at _____. It's important to me that you don't get behind, and I also want to minimize distractions for the other students, once we have started." This reinforces expectations and helps to show that the behavior affects not only them but also the other students.

3. Collaboration:

Ask the student what is happening before class that makes it hard for them to get to class on time and ask if there is anything you can do to help. Say, "Let's try to make every effort to be here on time tomorrow. You got this." Thank the student for listening.

Note: This conversation should be held in private.

Scenario 5: A Student is Being Bullied (Addressing the Victim)

1. Connection:

Speak to the victim privately, displaying empathy. Address the student by name and say, "I saw what happened to you, and I want to make sure you're okay. What are you feeling right now?"
This shows genuine care and concern.

2. Communication:

Acknowledge their feelings and reassure them that you want to help. Say, "What Johnny (i.e., say that student's name) did and/or said was hurtful, and you didn't deserve to be treated that way. It's my responsibility to make sure you feel safe and respected in our class." This lets the student know that you take bullying seriously.

3. Collaboration:

Work with the student to come up with a plan. Say, "Let's work together to come up with a plan to make sure you are comfortable in this class. If this happens again, I want you to let me know so we can handle it together." Ask the student what they need from you that might help. *Note: Report the incident to the appropriate school administrator and/or counselor. This might not be the first time.*

Scenario 6: A Student is Bullying Others (Addressing the Bully)

1. **Connection:**

    To avoid shaming the bully, speak with them in private. Address the student by name and say, "Tell me about what I saw happen earlier with you and _____ (Student's Name). What led to those actions?" This is an attempt to provide the student with a moment of reflection and an attempt to get to the root cause of the behavior.

2. **Communication:**

    In a non-threatening manner, let the bully know that their behavior is not acceptable and that it is harmful to others. Address the student by name and say, "What you did made (Student's Name) feel unsafe, and that is not ok. Our classroom is a safe space for everyone, including you." This allows you to hold the student accountable without shaming or attacking their character. (Disciplining with Dignity)

3. Collaboration:

Say, "What do you need to do to help you manage your emotions in the future so that you do not continue to engage in this behavior, so you avoid the consequences for this type of behavior? Know that if something is frustrating you, I'm here for you, too."

The goal is to get the student who is bullying others to take responsibility for their actions, model an appropriate way to deal with conflict, and help keep your relationship with the student intact. *Note: Report the incident to the appropriate school administrator and/or counselor. This might not be the first time.*

The six examples provided using the C³ Key Principles™ represent a small number of the types of disruptive behaviors that take place in and outside the classroom. However, they provide an intentional framework for communicating expectations while redirecting inappropriate behavior in a consistent, non-threatening, and non-judgmental way.

Remember, as educators, you are always teaching, and appropriate modeling is always a great lesson. 😊

Chapter Four Key Takeaways

1. Emotional Intelligence helps with classroom management and discipline.

2. Disciplinary moments can turn into learning opportunities for managing emotions.

3. When addressing discipline, modeling intentional strategies can redirect behavior, build trust, and equip students with emotional and responsible decision-making skills.

Reflection Exercise

Ask Yourself:

- How can I incorporate emotional intelligence into my classroom management practices to address disruptive behavior?

- Which aspect of the C³ Key Principles™ (i.e., Connection, Communication, and Collaboration) can I strengthen to help me in addressing discipline?

- Think of a challenging behavior from past experiences—how could using the C³ Key Principles™ have changed the outcome for me and/or the student?

CHAPTER FIVE

C³ EQED Classroom Resources

> *"Concentrate all your thoughts upon the work in hand. The sun's rays do not burn until brought to a focus."*
> **- Alexander Bell**

Planning is an integral part of the teaching and learning process. Schools have all types of plans to ensure student success—strategic, operational, curriculum, lesson, behavior, and the infamous school improvement plan, to name a few. Each of these is necessary to ensure student success, and while it goes without saying that students can't learn in a chaotic environment, it is also true that it is hard for students to learn from teachers where there is no connection. This is why having a classroom management plan that includes building relationships with students is just as important as any other type of planning.

The C³ Key Principles™ provide a structured and intentional framework to build relationships with your students while modeling for them how to make meaningful connections with one another.

This section provides resources that promote emotional management while creating engaging, reflective learning environments for you and your students. These interactions have the power to transform the culture of any environment into a space and place where everyone thrives. Use these resources to help you create a classroom management plan that includes intentional practices to help connect, communicate, and collaborate with your students to transform the learning process.

The Power C Chart™

The Power C Chart™ is an extension of the C³ Key Principles™. This resource is a visual tool that helps you plan for intentional efforts to build connections, strengthen communication, and enhance collaboration in the classroom. The Power C Chart™ can help you identify consistent patterns of behaviors to foster positive, safe learning environments where everyone is seen, valued, heard, and celebrated.

A list of intentional strategies to build meaningful connections, improve communication, and foster collaboration in your daily instructional practices and interactions has been provided. From the examples, select the ones you plan to use or ones you currently use and write them in the appropriate category. As you learn new strategies, add them to the chart on the following page for even more intentional moments of connection, communication, and collaboration in your daily classroom procedures, routines, and interactions.

- **Connection:**
    o Smile
    o Greet Students *SEE ME Framework™
    o Say, "Thank you."
    o Affirm Desired Behavior (e.g., Give Praise)
    o Celebrate Student Success

- **Communication:**
  - Listen
  - Repeat What You Heard
  - Post Objectives and Expectations
  - Ask Questions
  - Give Clear Instructions

- **Collaboration:**
  - Assign Group Projects
  - Incorporate Student-Led Discussions
  - Create a Class Motto
  - Give Choices

The Power C Chart™

Intentional Ways to Creating Engaging Environments

CONNECTION	COMMUNICATION	COLLABORATION
Smile	Listen	Assign Group Roles

The Keep, Stop, Start Tool

The Keep, Stop, Start Tool is a powerful reflective tool that helps individuals and teams evaluate their performance and is useful in any setting. This tool offers great insight into behaviors, which proves to be extremely helpful for teachers' personal and professional growth. The Keep, Stop, Start Tool provides a lens through which educators can get insight into what's working in their classrooms, what's not, and what needs to be considered. *Tip: Use it to reflect on your implementation of the C³ Key Principles™.*

Here are the instructions for using the Keep, Stop, Start as a personal reflective tool:

- **Keep**: Identify practices that work well and that you should continue in your classroom. This can be everything from how the day starts to how you connect, communicate, and collaborate with your students. *Think about what you do that positively impacts your students and contributes to a healthy, emotionally intelligent classroom environment.*

- **Stop**: Reflect on your current teaching practices and your interactions with your students. What are some things you need to stop doing because they are getting in the way of your ability to connect with students or they cause confusion? *Think about how you communicate and share information with your students.*

- **Start**: Identify new strategies or approaches that provide clarity and help to build connections—creating a sense of safety and belonging. These might be ideas from earlier chapters or new ones you plan to use.

Example:

- **Keep**: Greeting students.

- **Stop**: Reacting too quickly or overreacting when students disrupt the class.

- **Start**: Taking a moment to breathe and check your emotions before addressing students.

Using the Keep, Stop, Start Tool is a great way to foster continuous improvement and provide clear communication in the classroom. Use it with the class to have students reflect on whole group behaviors. You can also have students use it to reflect on their own personal behaviors. The Keep, Stop, Start Tool empowers students to take an active role in shaping their classroom culture. The tool is a great conversation starter for classroom meetings.

Classroom meetings look different for elementary and secondary teachers regarding seating arrangement and how many topics are discussed at once. An example has been provided, but be sure to use your professional judgment to decide whether to discuss each item all at once or break them into multiple conversations over an extended period of time.

Example:

- **Keep:** Ask the students to name routines and ways of doing things that the class should keep doing because they work well. Ask them to name specific behaviors that happen in the classroom that make the classroom feel welcoming and positive.

- **Stop:** Ask students to share behaviors the class should stop doing because they hinder progress and make others feel disrespected or unsafe.

- **Start:** Have students name behaviors the class can start doing to create a more welcoming, engaging environment. Be sure to have them name specific behaviors.

Be sure to capture the students' responses on the chart. (See Appendix for blank Keep, Stop, Start Chart.)

C³ Key Principles™ EQed Implementation Management Plan

Creating an engaging environment in the classroom requires a commitment to ongoing reflection and intentional action. Developing a C³ Key Principles™ EQed Implementation Management Plan can help you implement systems and practices that will enhance your emotional management while modeling for and teaching students what Social and Emotional Learning Skills look like in action effectively in your classroom.

The C³ Key Principles™ EQed Implementation Management Plan helps you plan and put everything you have learned into action. It's a great tool for setting short-term and long-term goals. The goal is not trying to work on everything all at once so you can check the box and say, "I did that," but rather to choose a focus area and work on that area for a period of time so that it becomes a natural part of your interactions with your students.

The C³ Key Principles EQed Implementation Management Plan

Revisit The C³ Key Principles™ and decide which area you want to begin to work on first. Write your focus area on the line below.

The C³ Key Principles™:
Connection, Communication, and Collaboration

Focus Area_____

For your area of focus, which activity will you implement first? This can be something you are already doing, but you need to be more consistent. Refer to your Power C Chart™ examples.

Activity_____

How will implementing this activity help to create a more engaging environment?

Answer these remaining questions as you plan for implementation:

- When will I do this activity?
- Where will I do this activity?
- How often will I do this activity?

Be sure to monitor both your students' reactions and your reactions to the process. Here are some questions to consider as you reflect on the process.

Reflection Considerations

Ask Yourself:

- How did it feel?
- How did my students respond?

- What else did I observe?

- What surprised me the most?

- What, if anything, needs to be adjusted?

See Appendix for a blank C³ Key Principles™ EQed Implementation Management Plan.

Chapter Five Key Takeaways

1. Personal reflection is a natural and necessary part of personal and professional growth.

2. Growing your emotional intelligence is a continuous process. It does not happen overnight. Take one step at a time.

3. Planning ways to intentionally connect, communicate, and collaborate with students helps to create engaging learning environments.

Reflection Exercise

Ask Yourself:

- What can I do today that will positively impact my class tomorrow?
- Which tool or resource will I use first?
- What other tools or resources do I need to explore?

CHAPTER SIX

SEL AND EQUITY: CREATING FAIR, ENGAGING, AND SUPPORTIVE ENVIRONMENTS

> *"SEL empowers us to connect, communicate and collaborate with others. Celebrating diversity allows see, understand, and appreciate one another."*
> **- Dr. Phyllis Donatto**

Social and Emotional Learning (SEL) and equity go hand in hand when it comes to creating engaging environments. SEL helps students develop important skills, both personal and professional, while equity ensures that every student gets what they need to succeed, no matter their background or circumstances. Using SEL as a lens to promote equity is a way to ensure that every student has a voice and feels like they belong.

Teachers can empower students to embrace diversity, navigate conflict, and contribute positively to their classrooms and communities by considering equity in SEL practices. Together, the two reinforce efforts to create classrooms where students can thrive in all areas of their lives by breaking down barriers that might hold them back. When educators integrate SEL with equity considerations, they create spaces for students to not only develop essential life skills but also experience fairness, respect, and belonging.

Equity Considerations with Actionable Steps:

1. Intentionally build trusting, mutually respectful, and caring relationships with students.

   Strategies to Consider:

   - Regular check-ins with students and families, acknowledging their unique experiences and perspectives.

- Dedicating time to learning more about students and their families through surveys, casual conversations, and/or home visits.
- Incorporate students' cultural and personal backgrounds into the classroom environment to celebrate diversity and inclusivity.

2. When issuing consequences, emphasize repairing harm, rebuilding relationships, and strengthening the class community.

    - Encourage students to take accountability for their actions while avoiding punitive measures.
    - Introduce restorative practices like reflection journals or one-on-one conferences where students can process their actions, understand their impact, and work toward repairing relationships.

3. Form positive relationships with students and create affirming student-centered classrooms.

    - Building rapport with students through active listening, encouragement, and inclusive practices.

- Set aside regular time for intentional relationship-building activities, such as morning meetings and sharing circles.

By combining SEL and equity, teachers can break down barriers, inspire learning, and help students succeed in and out of the classroom. These approaches ensure every student feels supported and has the chance to reach their full potential in a safe and inclusive environment.

Actionable steps like building trusting relationships, focusing on restorative practices, and fostering student-centered classrooms bring this vision to life. When teachers intentionally connect with their students, honor their unique experiences, and create spaces for accountability and growth, they pave the way for a classroom culture where every student feels seen, supported, and empowered to succeed.

Conclusion

As a teacher, your impact goes far beyond delivering content or preparing students for exams. You are shaping lives, fostering emotional growth, and modeling the skills that students will carry with them into the future. Emotional intelligence is at the heart of this work. By committing to developing your EQ, you are improving your teaching practice and creating a classroom environment where students feel safe, supported, and inspired to achieve their full potential.

Throughout this book, we've explored the impact that emotional intelligence can have on you, your classroom, and your students. By cultivating EQ in your teaching practice, you can improve your classroom management, build relationships with your students, and address disruptive behaviors in a non-threatening, relational manner. This approach has the power to not only help you and your students grow emotionally but also increase their chances for academic success.

As you continue developing your emotional intelligence, remember that growth comes through regularly reflecting on your classroom experiences, adjusting your approach based on those reflections, and trying again. Your commitment to growth can improve the emotional intelligence and well-being of both you and your students.

Let's revisit some key takeaways from the EQed Classroom:

1. **Growth Starts with Self-Awareness:** Knowing your strengths, where you struggle, and how you respond is the first step to creating meaningful interactions with your students. From the knowing, you can commence to growing.

2. **Connections Build Trust:** Forming connections is where trust begins with your students. When students feel safe and supported, they can become the best version of themselves by engaging in

class discussions, interacting with others positively, taking risks, and accepting redirection.

3. **Communication Matters**: "It's not what you say; it's how you say it." Intentional communication is essential for building relationships and creating a positive learning environment.

4. **Collaboration Empowers**: Empowering students through collaboration—giving them a voice and choice — helps them take ownership of their learning and develop critical social skills.

5. **Emotional Intelligence & Social and Emotional Learning are Different:** Emotional Intelligence & Social and Emotional Learning differ, yet they share the same goal. That is to help adults and students be the best version of themselves for themselves and others. Teachers who model emotional management help students develop the skills to handle their own emotions, reducing classroom disruptions and promoting a positive atmosphere.

For a more in-depth personalized or Team EQ Journey, schedule your professional development session today by contacting us at info@fthdimensions.com.

About the Author

Dr. **Phyllis Donatto** is the founder and CEO of FTH Dimension Solutions, a training, consulting, and executive leadership coaching firm specializing in empowerment solutions for professional and personal growth. She is also the founder of the i-MPACT | i-LEAD Foundation, a non-profit organization that empowers young adults to position their lives for greater impact through the power of self-awareness.

Dr. Donatto has extensive K-12 and post-secondary experience having served as an Assistant Professor of Curriculum and Instruction, PK-16+ Coordinator, Campus Improvement Specialist, Assistant Principal, Title 1 Compliance Coordinator, and Classroom Teacher.

Prior to launching her company, FTH Dimension Solutions, she served as Leadership Development Strategist for a leading national education training company and worked as an independent consultant.

Dr. Donatto is a certified TalentSmart Mastering EQ® Trainer with extensive leadership development and curriculum experience. Her exceptional coaching abilities and contributions have been recognized with the Coach Belin Award of Excellence and the President's Award for Transformational Coaching and Outstanding Leadership. She has presented nationally and internationally on the power of relationships in the workplace, social and emotional learning, and creating engaging environments.

Dr. Donatto has trained thousands across the United States, sharing her unique insights and practical tools for success. She is also an award-winning children's author, using her literary talents to inspire young minds. Her unwavering commitment to inspiring and uplifting others has earned her the title of "Hopeologist."

Dr. Donatto and her husband, Damond, have been married for 17 years. The two have one son, Ronald, and a grandson, Raphael.

Appendix

The Power C Chart™

Intentional Ways to Creating Engaging Environments

CONNECTION	COMMUNICATION	COLLABORATION
Smile	Listen	Assign Group Roles

@2020 FTH Dimension Solutions. All Rights Reserved.

DR. PHYLLIS DONATTO

Benefits of CASEL Competencies

 **SELF-AWARENESS**

DEFINITION: The ability to understand one's own emotions, thoughts, and values and how they influence behavior across contexts. *Collaborative for Academic, Social, and Emotional Learning (CASEL)* www.casel.org

BENEFITS:

- Articulate thoughts and feelings.
- Manage emotions appropriately.
- Understand how behaviors impact others.
- Recognize strengths and areas of growth.
- Recognize the needs of others.
- Create a plan for improvement.
- Possess resilience.

*These skills influence performance and increase chances for success.

WAYS TO GROW:

- Set goals and monitor progress.
- Ask for feedback.
- Take a Personality Assessment.
- Self-assess and reflect: Record thoughts in your Reflection Journal.

SOURCES & ADDITIONAL RESOURCES:

Ashley, Greg & Reiter-Palmon, Roni. (2012). Self-awareness and the evolution of leaders: The need for a better measure of self-awareness. Journal of Behavioral and Applied Management, 14, 2-17. 10.1037/t29152-000.
CASEL-SEL-Framework-11.2020.pdf
Goleman, D. (2014). *Emotional Intelligence: Why It Can Matter More Than IQ*. Bloomsbury Publishing.
Self-Awareness. (2021, January 08). Retrieved January 29, 2021, from https://mylearningtools.org/self-awareness/

©2020 FTH Dimension Solutions, LLC. All Rights Reserved.

THE EQED CLASSROOM

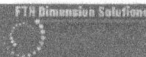 # SELF-MANAGEMENT

DEFINITION: The ability to manage one's emotions, thoughts, and behaviors effectively in different situations to achieve goals and aspirations. *Collaborative for Academic, Social, and Emotional Learning (CASEL) www.casel.org*

BENEFITS:

- Engage in problem-solving.
- Increase productivity/performance.
- Recognize and manage emotions.
- Exercise self-control.

These skills influence performance and increase chances for success.

WAYS TO GROW:

- Set goals (i.e., daily, weekly, monthly).
- Develop and use a checklist.
- Gather materials in advance for meetings/lessons.
- Consider using wait time before responding.
- Plan for reflection.
- Evaluate progress.

SOURCES & ADDITIONAL RESOURCES:

CASEL-SEL-Framework-11.2020.pdf
Goleman, D. (2014). *Emotional Intelligence: Why It Can Matter More Than IQ.* Bloomsbury Publishing.
Power to the People: Why Self Management is important. (n.d.). Retrieved January 28, 2021, from
    https://er.educause.edu/blogs/2015/8/power-to-the-people-why-self-management-is-important
Self Management. (2021, January 08). Retrieved January 28, 2021, from
    https://mylearningtools.org/self-management/

©2020 FTH Dimension Solutions, LLC. All Rights Reserved.

SOCIAL AWARENESS

DEFINITION: The ability to understand the perspectives of and empathize with others, including those from diverse backgrounds, cultures, & contexts. *Collaborative for Academic, Social, and Emotional Learning (CASEL) www.casel.org*

BENEFITS:
- Build positive relationships.
- Exhibit leadership.
- Show empathy.
- Contemplate others' points of view.
- Listen.
- Solve conflict.

*These skills influence performance and increase chances for success.

WAYS TO GROW:
- Set goals and monitor progress.
- Ask for feedback.
- Take an EQ Assessment.
- Ask your friends questions about how you respond in certain situations.
- Self-assess and reflect: Record thoughts in your Reflection Journal.

SOURCES & ADDITIONAL RESOURCES:
CASEL-SEL-Framework-11.2020.pdf
Goleman, D. (2014). *Emotional Intelligence: Why It Can Matter More Than IQ.* Bloomsbury Publishing.
Greater Good in Education 2021. SEL for Students: Social Awareness and Relationship Skills | Greater Good in Education. [online] Available at: <https://ggie.berkeley.edu/student-well-being/sel-for-students-social-awareness-and-relationship-skills> [Accessed 28 January 2021]. SEL for Students: Social Awareness and Relationship Skills | Greater Good In Education (berkeley.edu).
How an Increased Social Awareness Creates Happy Relationships. (2020, September 15). Retrieved January 28, 2021, from https://donorcure.com/social-awareness/

RESPONSIBLE DECISION-MAKING

DEFINITION: The ability to make caring and constructive choices about personal behavior and social interactions across diverse situations and to evaluate the benefits and consequences of various actions for personal, social, and collective well-being. *Collaborative for Academic, Social, and Emotional Learning (CASEL) www.casel.org*

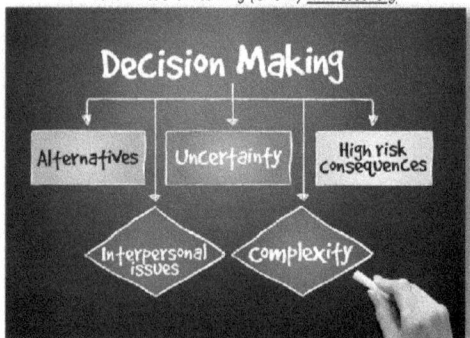

BENEFITS:

- Engage in problem-solving.
- Increase productivity/performance.
- Recognize and manages emotions.
- Exercise self-control.

*These skills influence performance and increase chances for success.

WAYS TO GROW:

- Use scenarios: *If this happens, then what?*
- Explore possible consequences.
- Consider how emotions influence decisions.
- Assess progress.

SOURCES & ADDITIONAL RESOURCES:

Achieving Goals & Making Decisions. (2020, December 08). Retrieved January 29, 2021, from https://mylearningtools.org/achieving-goals-making-decisions/
CASEL-SEL-Framework-11.2020.pdf
Goleman, D. (2014). *Emotional Intelligence: Why It Can Matter More Than IQ.* Bloomsbury Publishing. Responsible Decision Making (Social Emotional Learning). (2021, January 20). Retrieved January 28, 2021, from https://www.landmarkoutreach.org/strategies/responsible-decision-making/

DR. PHYLLIS DONATTO

RELATIONSHIP SKILLS

DEFINITION: The ability to establish and maintain healthy and supportive relationships and effectively navigate settings with diverse individuals and groups. *Collaborative for Academic, Social, and Emotional Learning (CASEL)* www.casel.org

BENEFITS:
- Build relationships and friendships.
- Collaborate and interact well with others.
- Engage in productive conflict.
- Communicate effectively.
- Exhibit leadership.
- Value others.

These skills influence performance and increase chances for success.

WAYS TO GROW:
- Learn the names of classmates/teammates.
- Spend time getting to know others (e.g., interests, hobbies, motivation, and aspirations).
- Ask questions.
- Laugh with others.
- Watch communication cues (i.e., facial expression, body language, tone of voice).
- Offer to help others with a problem/project.
- Be positive.

SOURCES & ADDITIONAL RESOURCES:

CASEL_SEL-Framework-1-2020.pdf
Goleman, D. (2011). Emotional Intelligence: *Emotional Intelligence: Why It Can Matter More Than IQ.*
Heather Kent. Heather Kent is the Regional Specialized 4-H Agent in the Northwest Extension District. (2021, January 22).
 Cultivating Communication Skills: Non-Verbal Cues. Retrieved January 29, 2021, from
 http://nwdistrict.ifas.ufl.edu/4hn/2021/01/22/cultivating-communication-skills-non-verbal-cues/
Relationship Skills. (2021, January 08). Retrieved January 29, 2021, from https://www.mindtools.org/relationship-skills/
The Mind Tools Content Team By the Mind Tools Content Team, T., Wrote, M., Wrote, A., & Wrote, B. (n.d.).
 Building Good Work Relationships: Making Work Enjoyable and Productive. Retrieved January 29, 2021, from
 https://www.mindtools.com/pages/article/good-relationships.htm

The EQed Classroom

The C³ Key Principles™
EQed Implementation Management Plan
Putting It Into Practice

Revisit The C³ Key Principles™ and choose the area where you'd like to start. Write your focus area and activity on the lines below.

The C³ Key Principles™ : Connection, Communication, and Collaboration

Focus Area _____

For your area of focus, which activity will you implement first?
This can be something you are already doing but may need to be more consistent. Refer to your The Power C Chart™ examples.

Actvity _____

How will implementing this activity help to create an engaging environment?

Answer these remaining questions as you plan for implementation.

When will you do this activity?

Where will you do this activity?

How often will you do this activit?y

Reflection Exercise

Ask Yourself:

How did it feel?

How did my students respond?

What else did I observe?

What surprised me the most?

What if anything needs to be adjusted?

@2020 FTH Dimension Solutions, LLC. All Rights Reserved.

Keep, Start, Stop Reflection

Sources

Brackett, M. A., & Rivers, S. E. (2014). *Transforming students' lives with social and emotional learning*. Yale Center for Emotional Intelligence.

Cavanagh, S. R., & Kennelly, A. D. (2015). *Creating safe learning environments: The role of student-teacher relationships in mitigating the effects of bullying on academic performance*. Learning and Instruction, 36, 46-55.

Cohen, E. G. (1994). *Restructuring the classroom: Conditions for productive small groups*. Review of Educational Research, 64(1), 1-35.

Durlak, J. A., Weissberg, R. P., Dymnicki, A. B., Taylor, R. D., & Schellinger, K. B. (2011). *The impact of enhancing students' social and emotional learning: A meta-analysis of school-based universal interventions*. Child Development, 82(1), 405-432.

Goleman, D. (1995). *Emotional intelligence: Why it can matter more than IQ*. Bantam Books.

Gross, J. J. (2015). *Emotion regulation: Current status and future prospects*. Psychological Inquiry, 26(1), 1-26.

Jennings, P. A., & Greenberg, M. T. (2009). *The prosocial classroom: Teacher social and emotional competence in relation to student and classroom outcomes*. Review of Educational Research, 79(1), 491–525.

Johnson, D. W., & Johnson, R. T. (2009). *An educational psychology success story: Social interdependence theory and cooperative learning*. Educational Researcher, 38(5), 365-379.

Marzano, R. J. (2003). *Classroom management that works: Research-based strategies for every teacher*. ASCD.

Zinsser, K. M., & Zinsser, A. (2016). *Teachers' emotion regulation and the development of young children's emotional competence*. Handbook of Emotional Development in Early Childhood Education, 327–344.

Tait, M. (2008). *Resilience as a contributor to novice teacher success, commitment, and retention.* Teacher Education Quarterly, 35(4), 57-75.

Pianta, R. C., Hamre, B. K., & Allen, J. P. (2012). *Teacher-student relationships and engagement: Conceptualizing, measuring, and improving the capacity of classroom interactions.* Handbook of Research on Student Engagement (pp. 365-386). Springer.

Petrides, K. V., & Furnham, A. (2001). *Trait emotional intelligence: Psychometric investigation with reference to established trait taxonomies.* European Journal of Personality, 15(6), 425-448.

Shriver, T. P., & Weissberg, R. P. (2005). *No emotion left behind.* Educational Leadership, 62(1), 16–21.

Sutton, R. E., & Wheatley, K. F. (2003). *Teachers' emotions and teaching: A review of the literature and directions for future research.* Educational Psychology Review, 15(4), 327-358.

Zins, J. E., Weissberg, R. P., Wang, M. C., & Walberg, H. J. (2004). *Building academic success on social and emotional learning: What does the research say?* Teachers College Press.

www.ingramcontent.com/pod-product-compliance
Lightning Source LLC
Chambersburg PA
CBHW040231110526
44582CB00001B/13